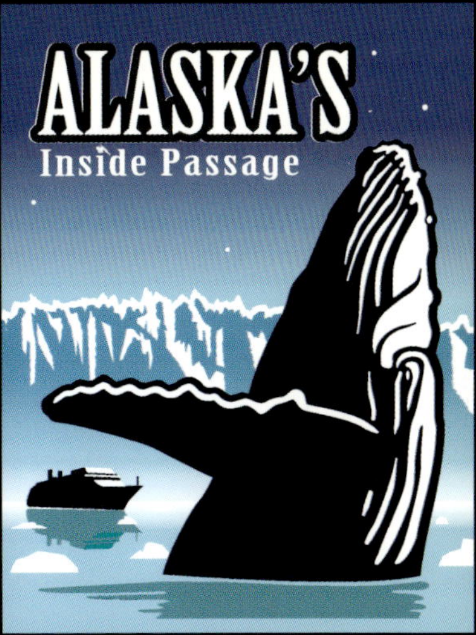

ALASKA'S
Inside Passage

Edited and Compiled by Carrie Compton
Cover Illustration by Dave Ember

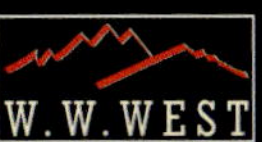

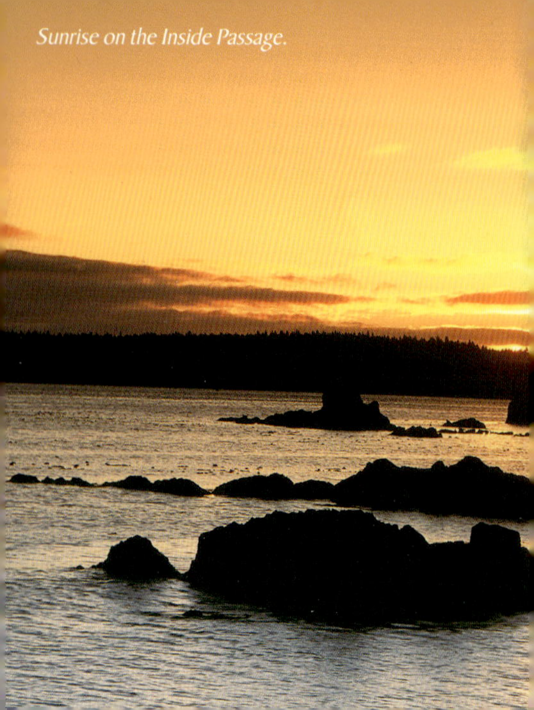

Sunrise on the Inside Passage.

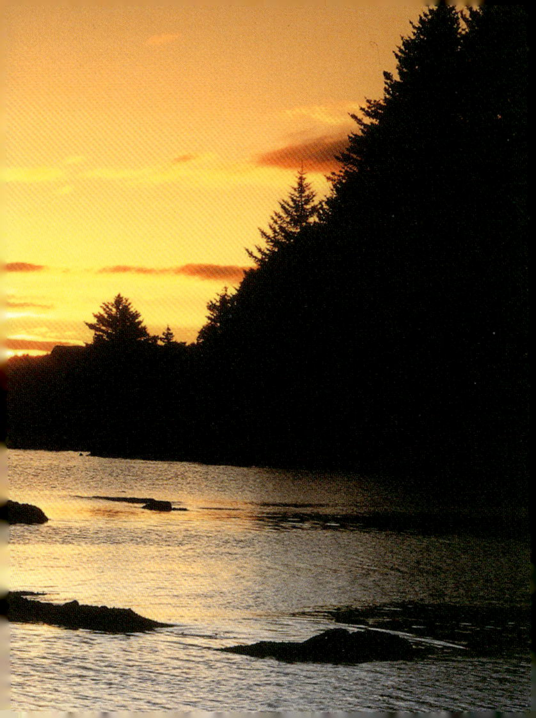

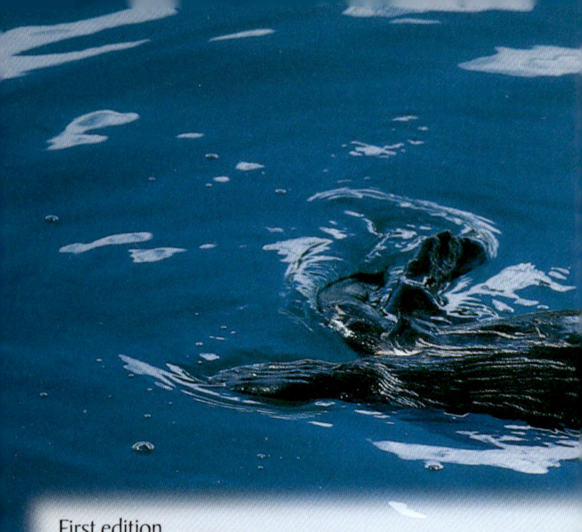

First edition
Published by W.W.West, Inc.
20875 Sholes Road
Bend, Oregon 97702
Book Design by Linda McCray
Cover Illustration by Dave Ember
Copy Editor: Barbara Fifer
Project Manager: Carrie Compton

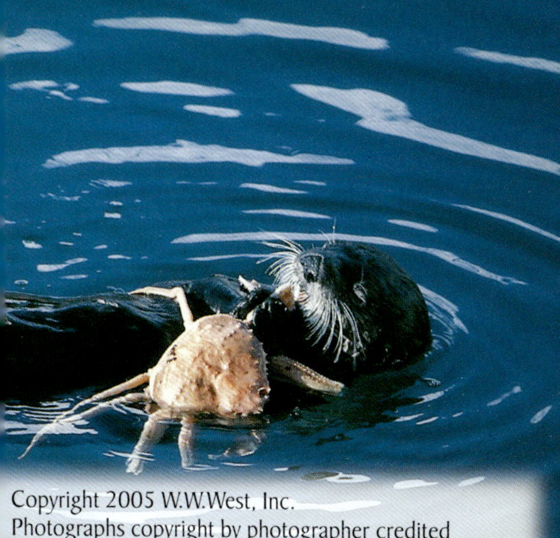

ISBN 0-9758960-0-8
Printed in China by C & C Offset Printing Company

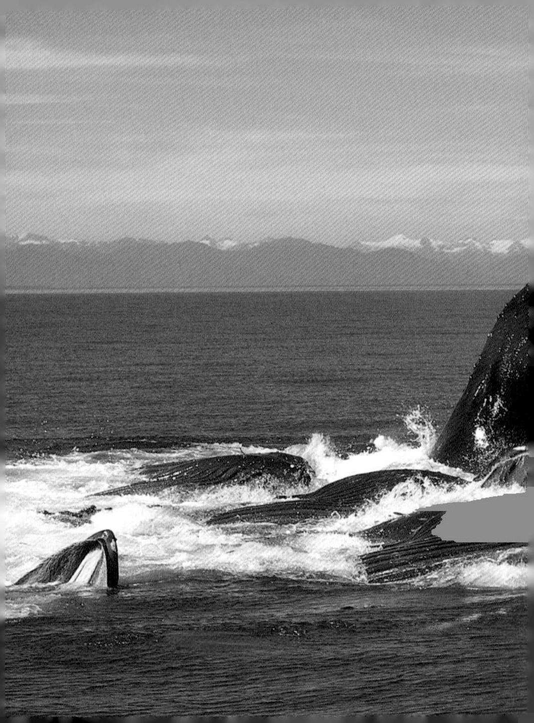

Humpback whales lunge feeding, which happens when their food is tightly grouped. Humpbacks lunge forward with their mouths opened wide.

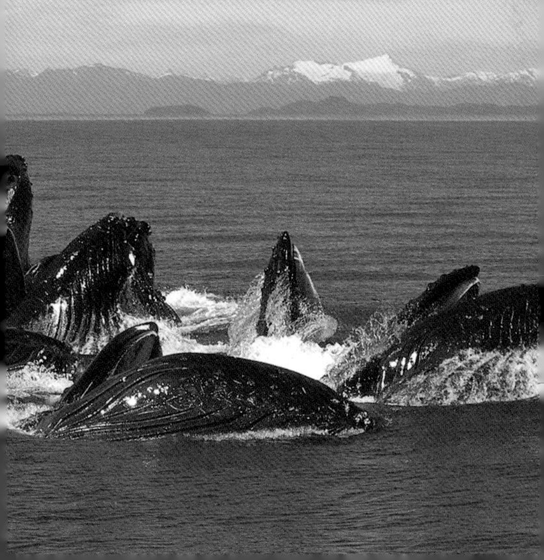

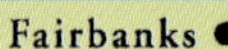

ALASKA

Anchorage

College Fjord

Alyeska Resort

Seward

PRINCE WILLIAM SOUND

KENAI FJORDS NATIONAL PARK

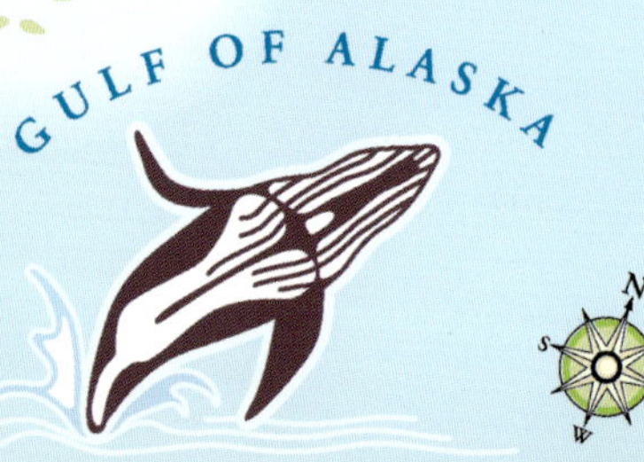

N

S

E

W

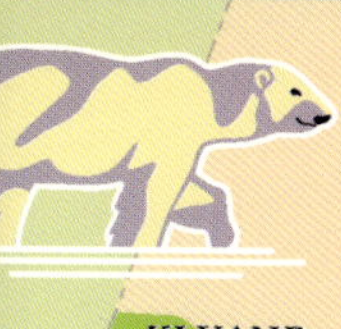

YUKON TERRITORY

KLUANE NATIONAL PARK

BRITISH COLUMBIA

Frasier

Skagway

Haines

Juneau

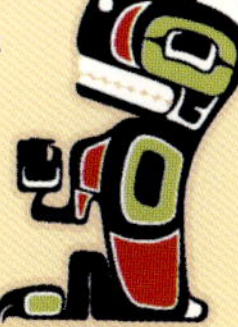

GLACIER BAY NATIONAL PARK

Sitka

SITKA NATIONAL HISTORICAL PARK

MISTY FJORDS NATIONAL MONUMENT

Ketchikan

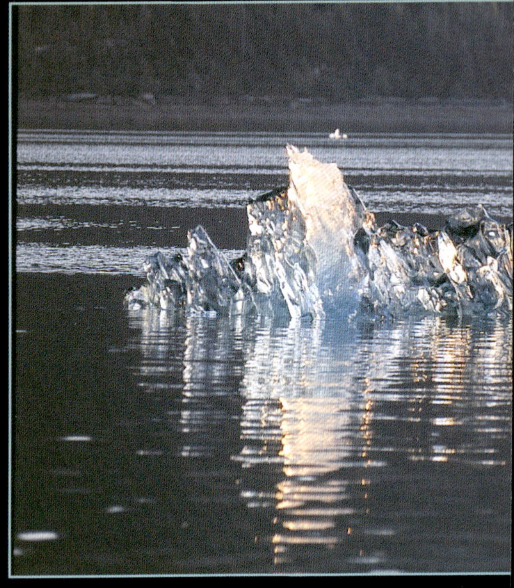

Ice floating by in the evening light.

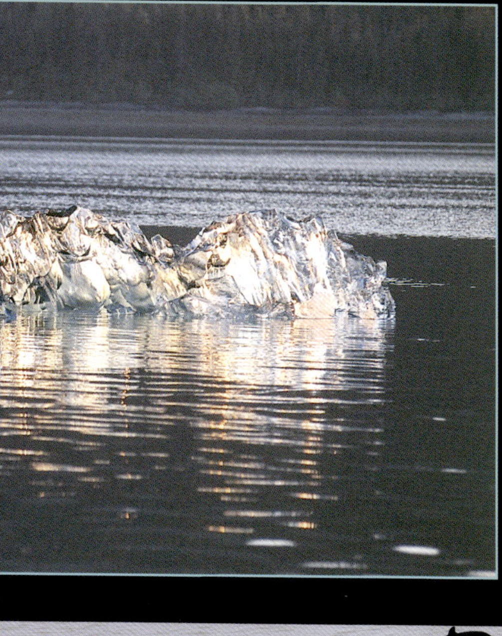

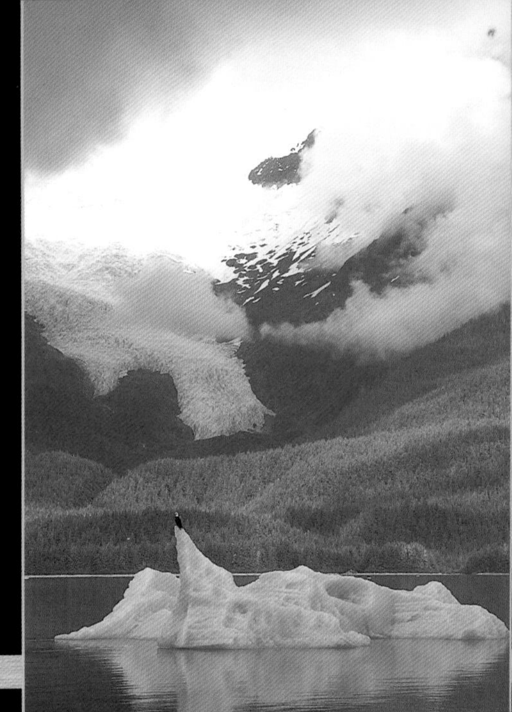

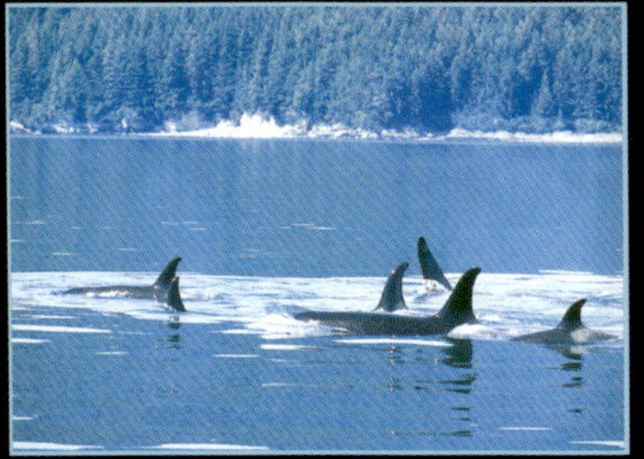

"Day after day, we seemed to float in a true fairyland, each succeeding view seeming more and more beautiful."

John Muir

A bald eagle rests on an iceberg.

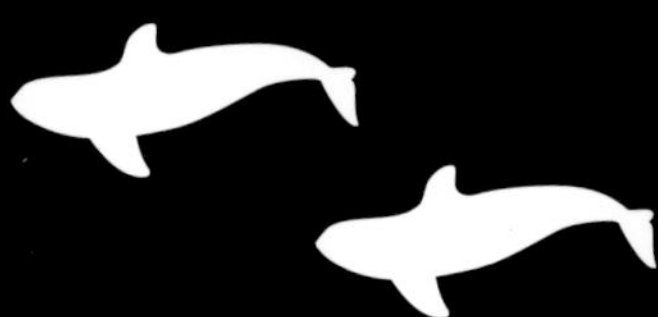

The Inside Passage; measured from the exit of Puget Sound in Washington State to the entrance of the Chilkat River near Haines, extends 1,000 miles.

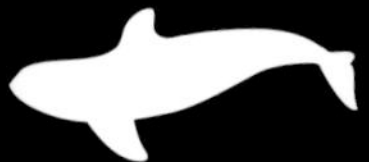

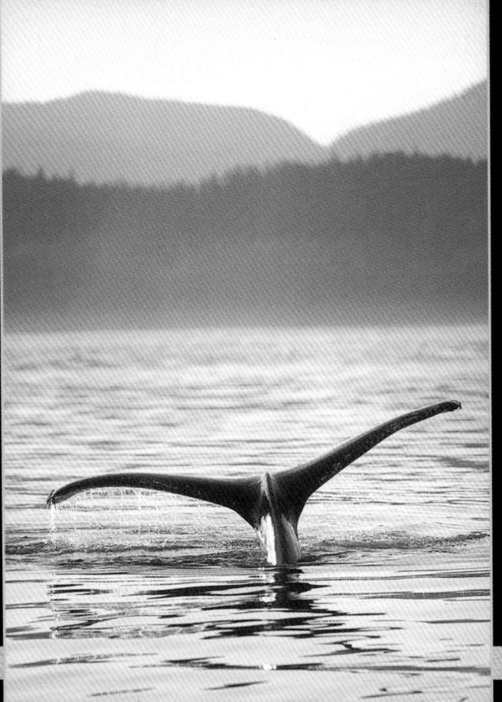

In the fall, along the Chilkat River, several thousand bald eagles gather to feed on salmon.

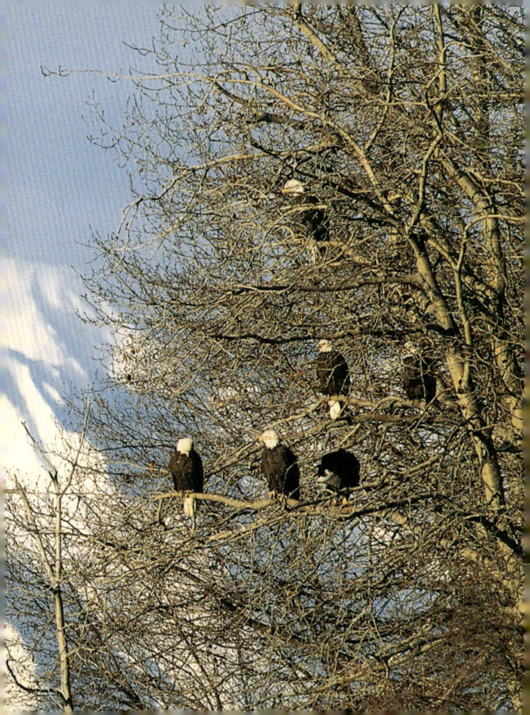

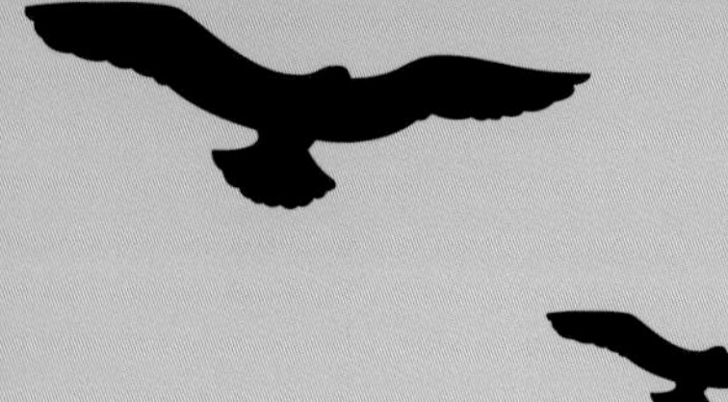

Within the Tongass National Forest is the largest number of nesting bald eagles in North America.

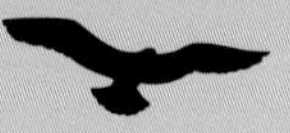

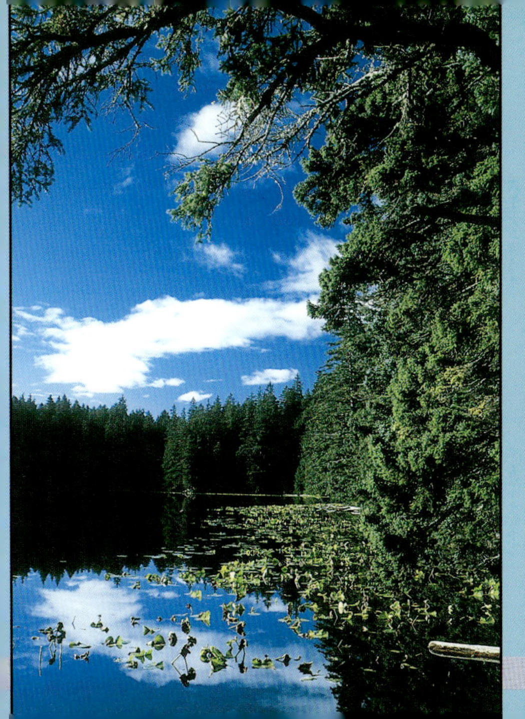

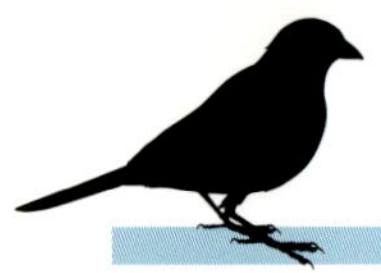

Alaska is a bird-watcher's paradise. It is estimated that more than 50 million birds nest along the vast Alaska coastline. The champion long-distance traveler is the Arctic tern, traveling 10,000 miles from Antarctica to nest in Alaska.

Artic Tern

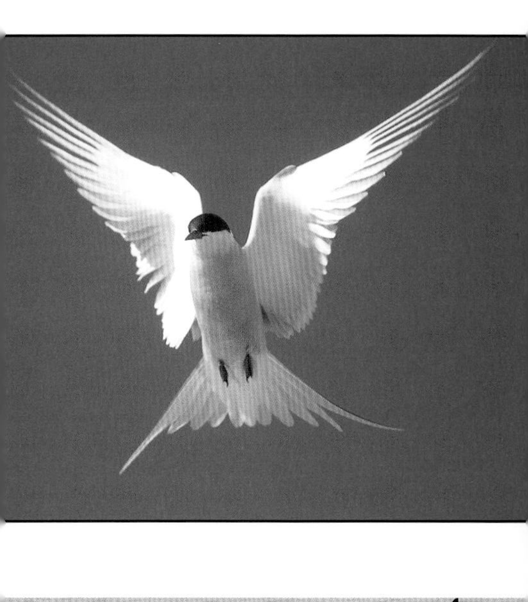

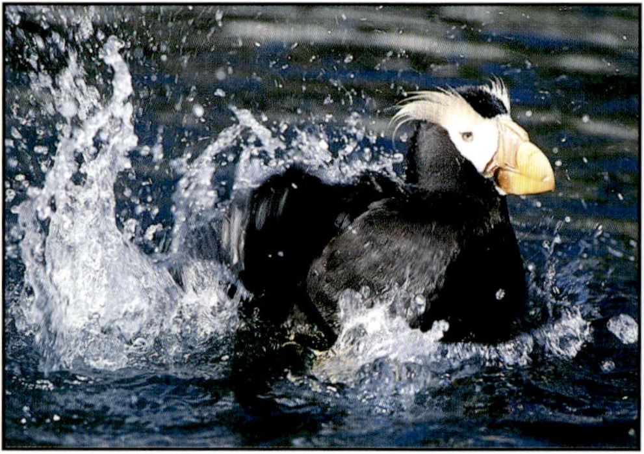

Tufted puffin.
Horned puffin.

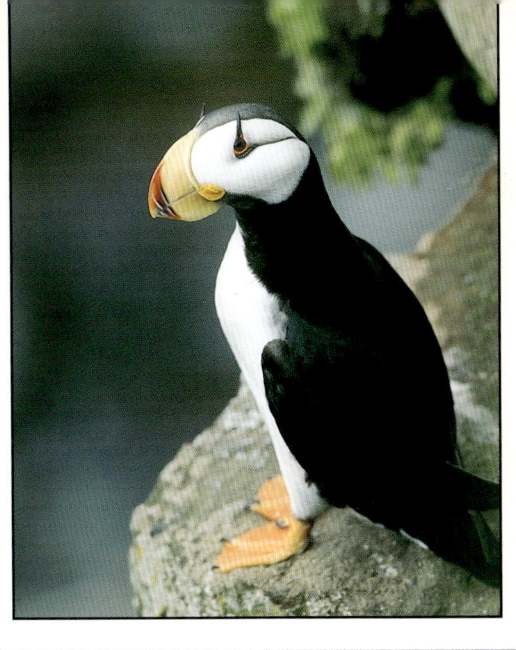

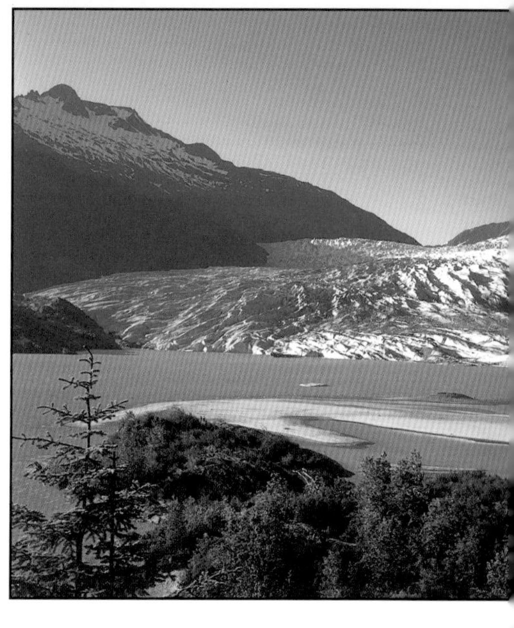

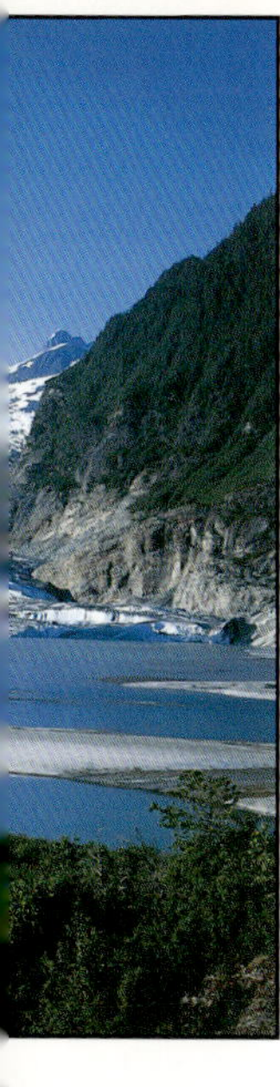

The Tongass National Forest, almost 17 million acres, is America's biggest national forest, and lies along the Inside Passage.

Mendenhall Glacier in Tongass National Forest.

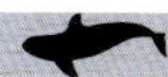

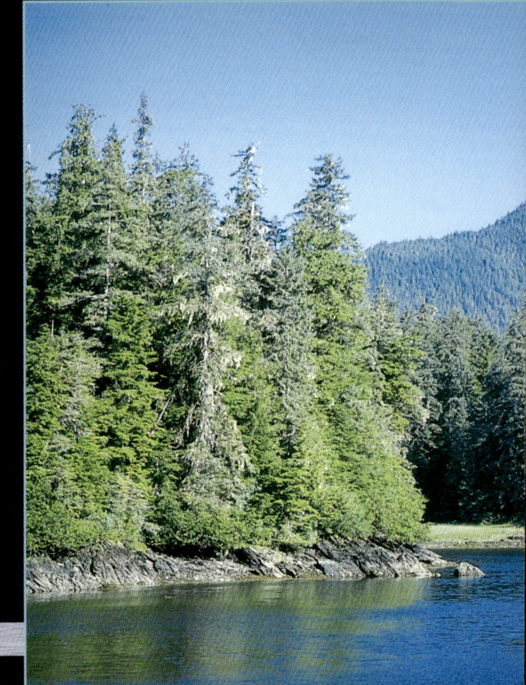

Traveling the Inside Passage is Alaska's most popular tourist route. The scenery is stunning and wildlife is everywhere, including a large population of brown bears on Admiralty Island.

A spawning stream on Admiralty Island.

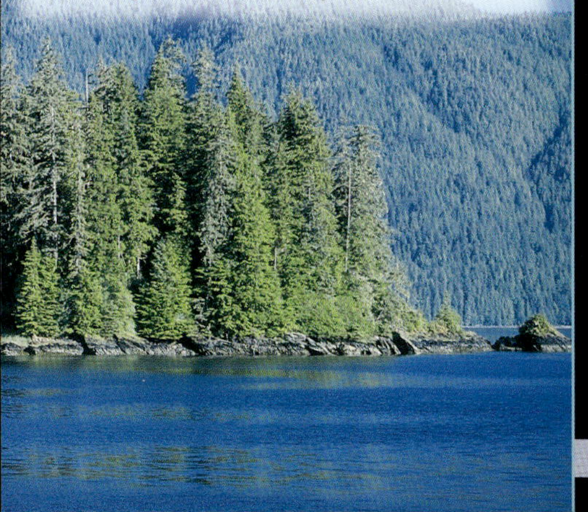

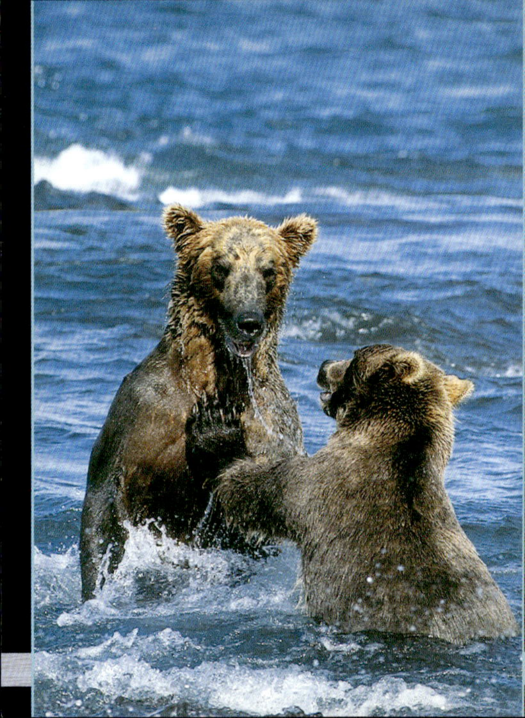

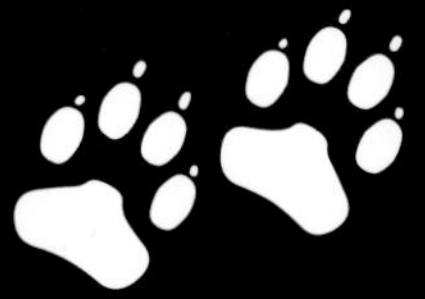

Admiralty Island earned the reputation of, "fortress of the bears," from the area's Tlinget tribe.

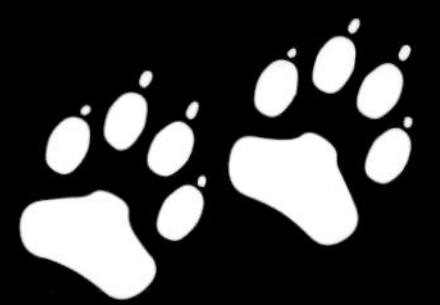

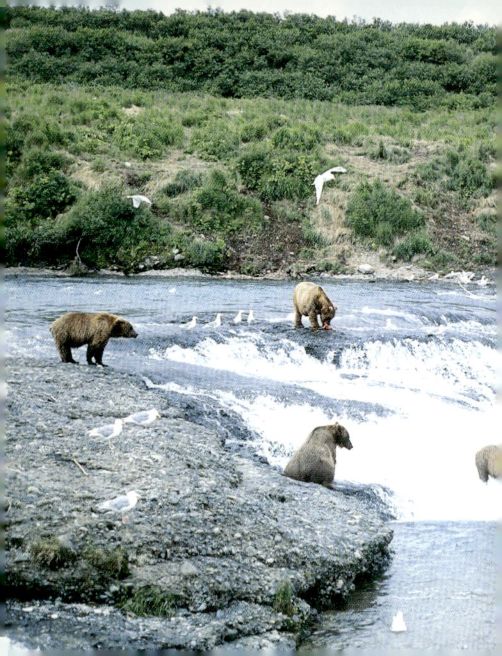

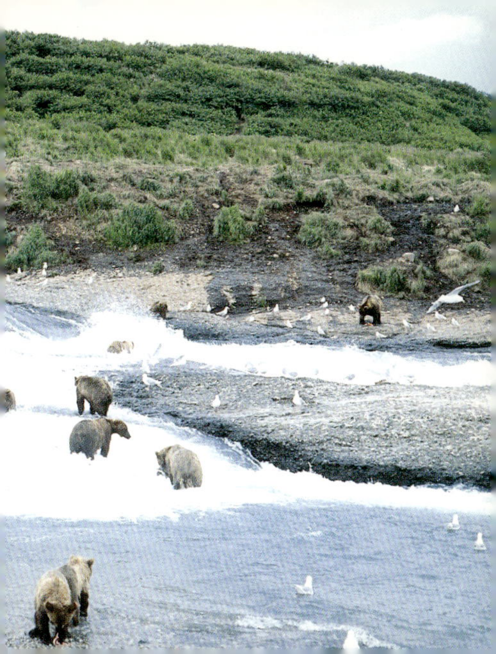

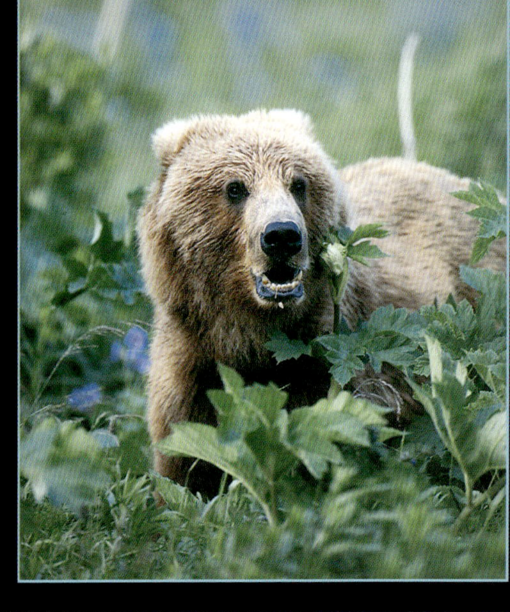

"A bear track at any time may create a stronger emotion than the old bear himself, for the imagination is brought into play. You examine the landscape sharply, expecting a bear on every slope as your quickened interest becomes eager and enterprising. The bear is somewhere, and may be anywhere. The country has become alive with a new, rich quality.

Adolph Murie, naturalist

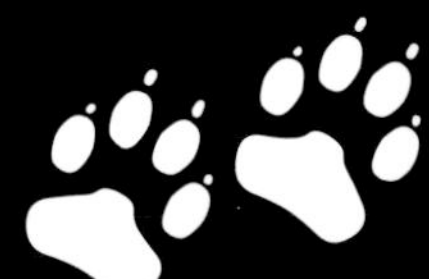

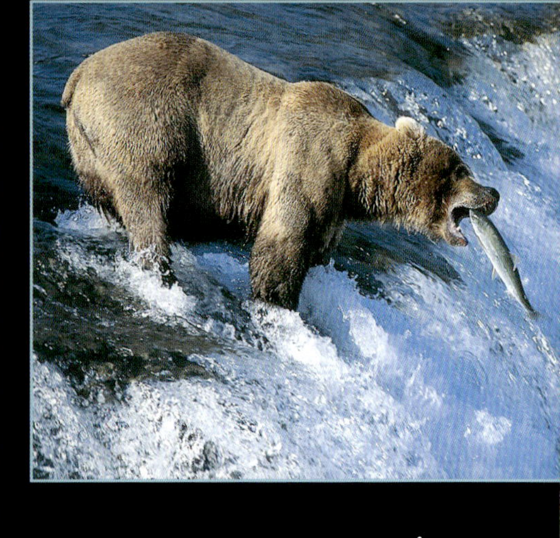

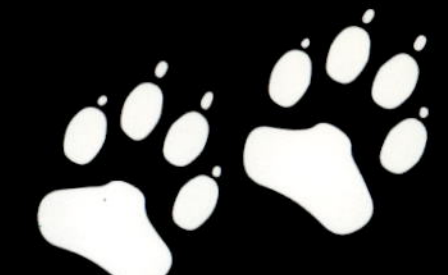

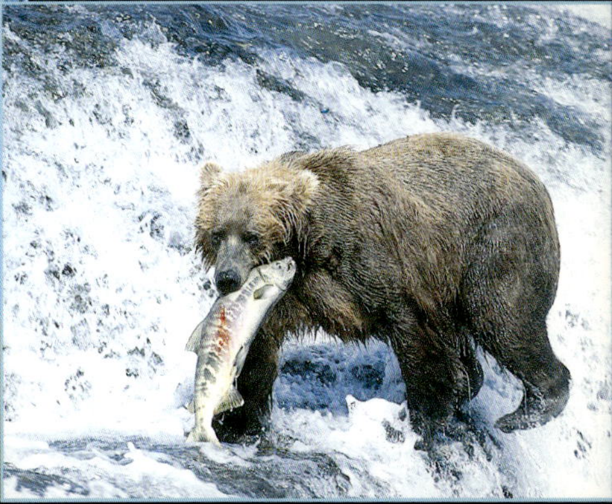

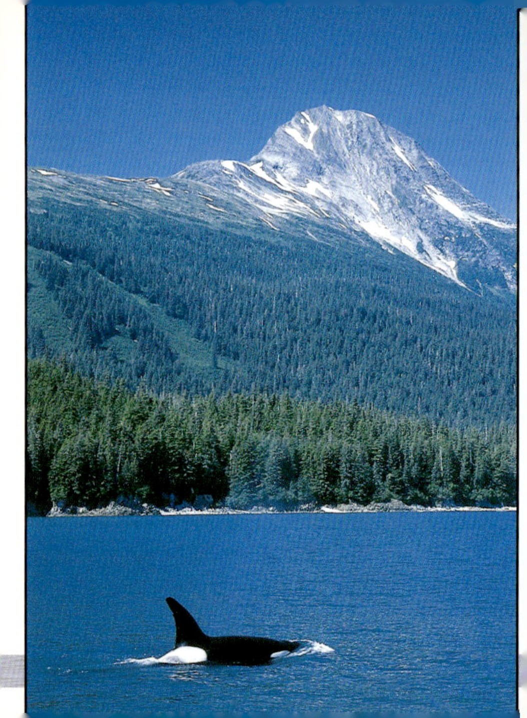

"You can never have enough of nature."

Henry David Thoreau

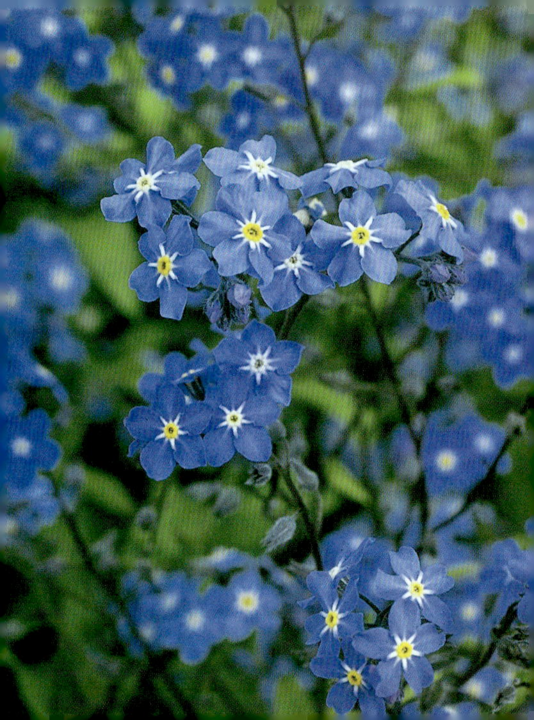

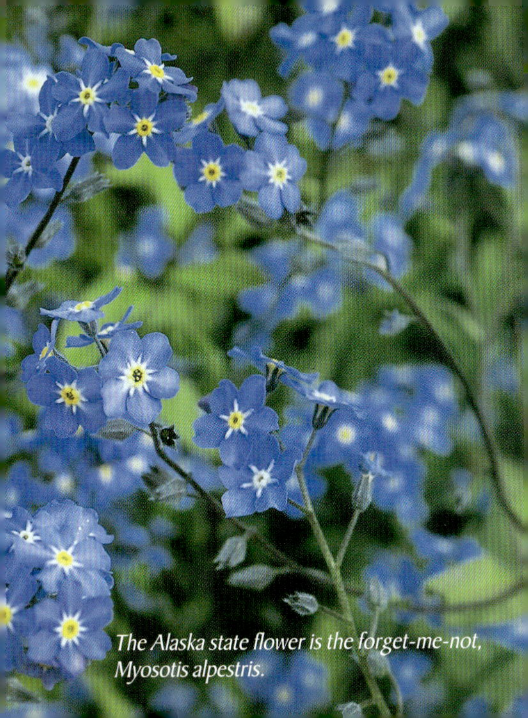

The Alaska state flower is the forget-me-not, Myosotis alpestris.

Alaska's extreme weather creates delightful miniature wildflower varieties scattered throughout the state. In the northern tundra, lovely 4" tall forget-me-not plants thrive.

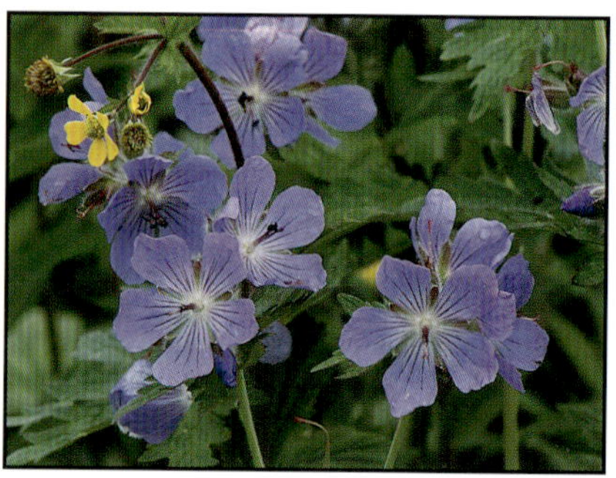

Wild geranium.

Wildflowers in Denali National Park.

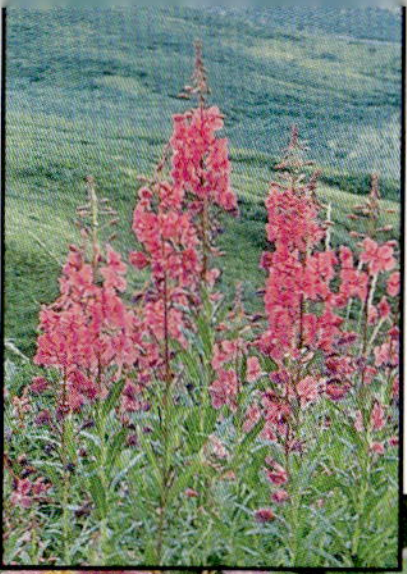

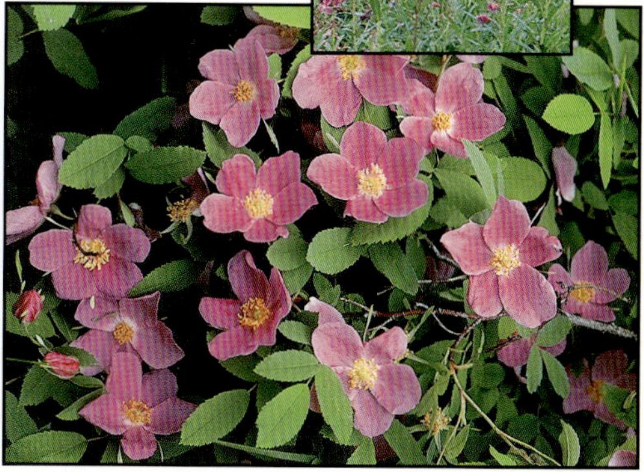

Prickly wild rose.

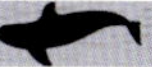

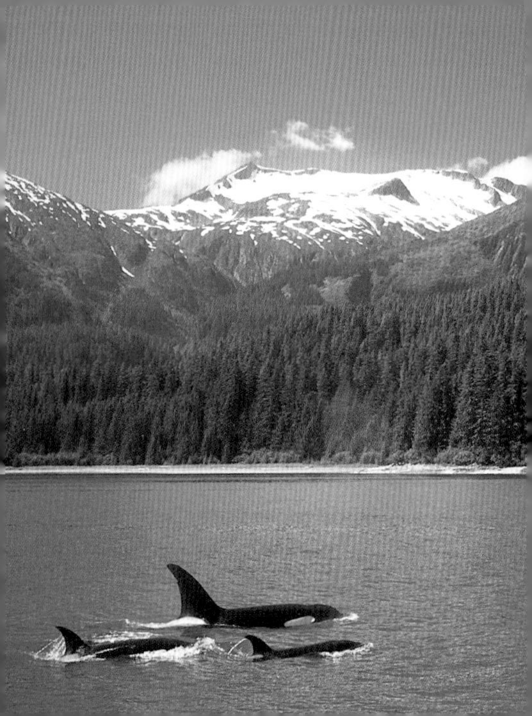

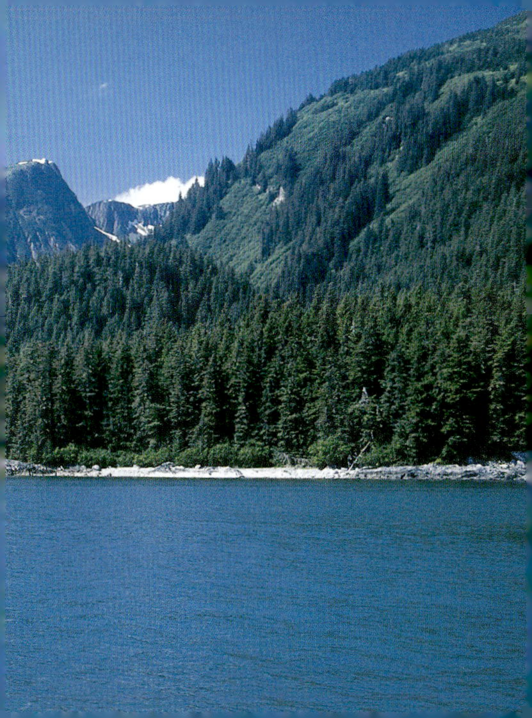

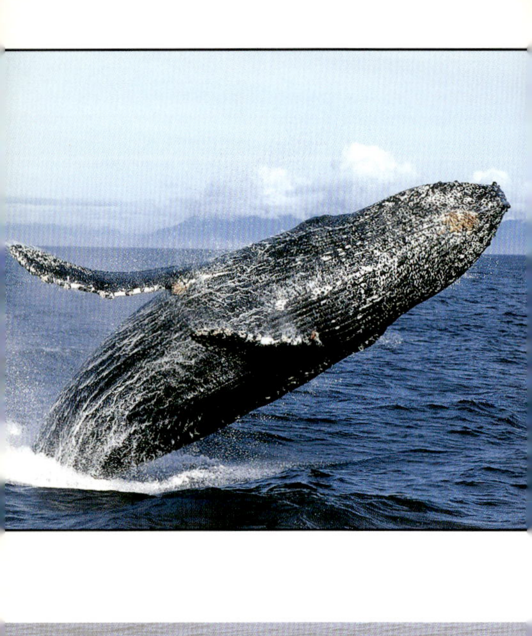

There are 17 species of whales, dolphins and porpoises in the waters of Alaska. Killer whales (orcas) are actually the largest member of the dolphin group.

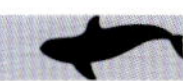

Seafood is Alaska's # 1 export and represents over 50% of America's production. Sportfishing enthusiasts travel from around the world to try their skill in Alaskan waters.

Salmon troller off Chicagof Island.

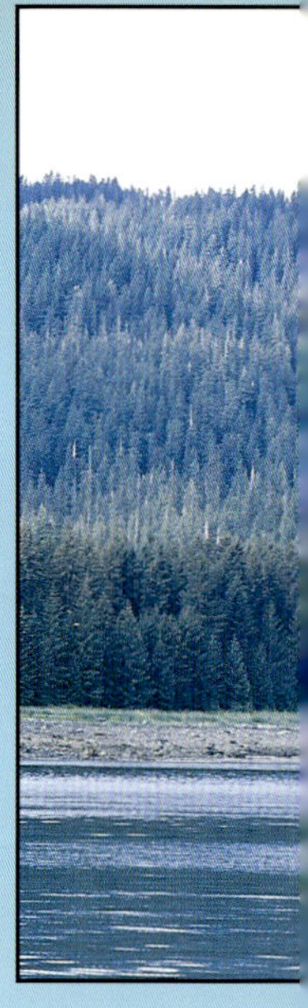

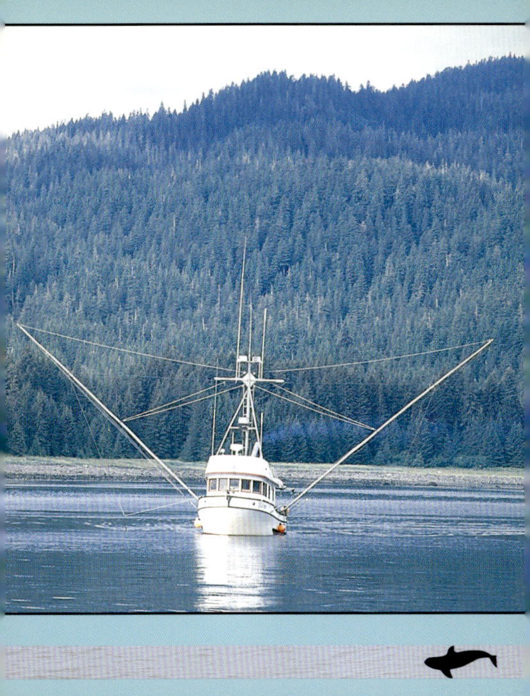

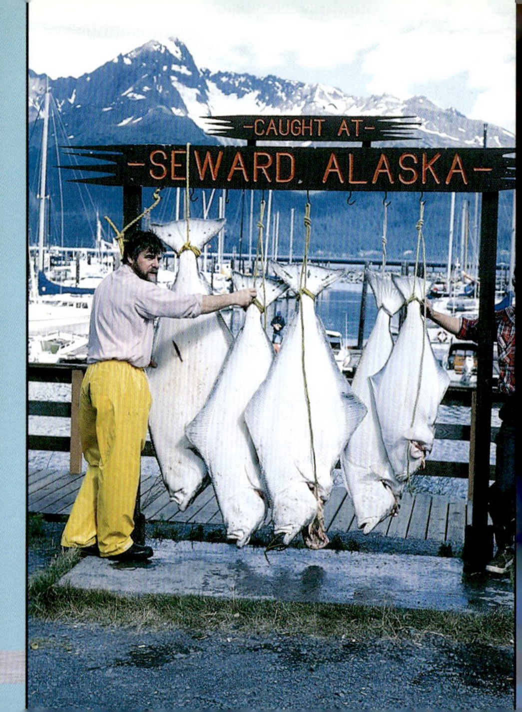
-CAUGHT AT-
-SEWARD ALASKA-

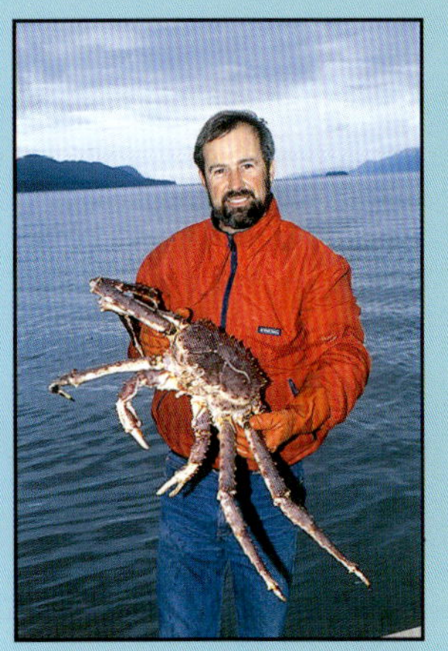

Alaska king crab.
Halibut sportfishing catch.

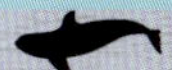

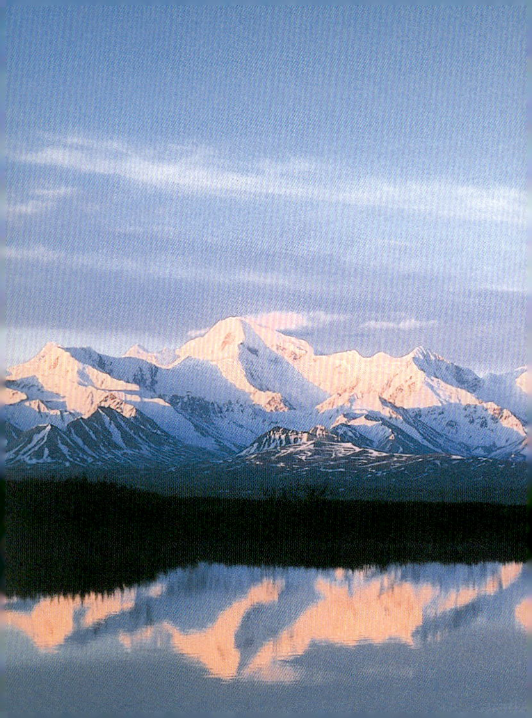

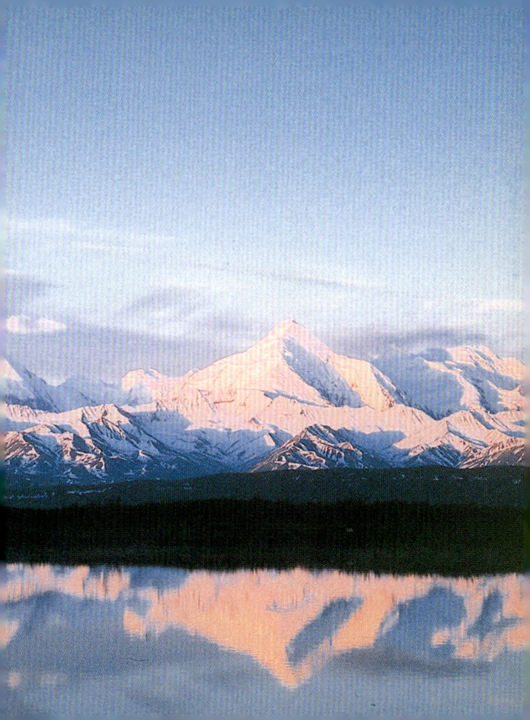

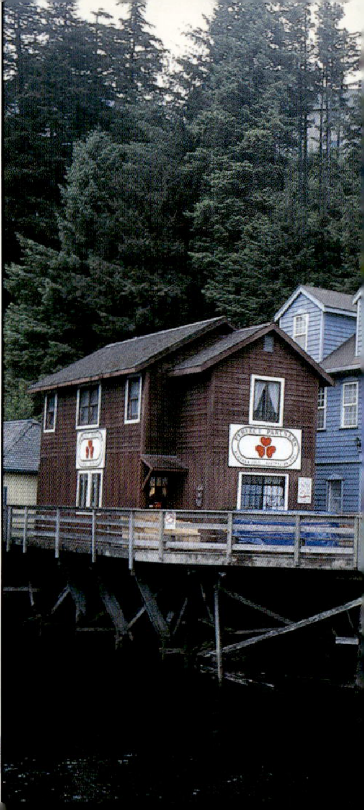

Creek Street, the one time "Red Light District" of Ketchikan, is now a respectable area of charming homes and gift shops. Robin Brandt

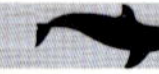

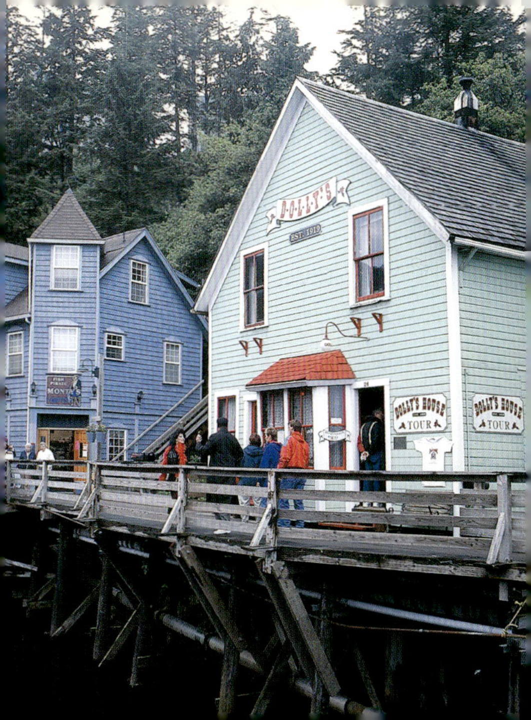
D·O·L·L·Y'S
EST. 1919
DOLLY'S HOUSE TOUR
DOLLY'S HOUSE TOUR

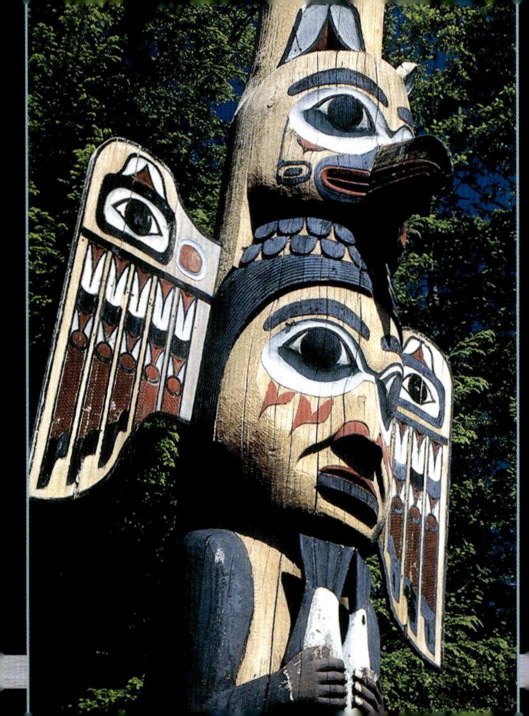

Ketchikan is the salmon capital of Alaska. Native peoples used images of the salmon in their ceremonial art. A humanized eagle is holding two salmon in this totem located in Ketchikan.

Clan House at Totem Bight State Park, Ketchikan.

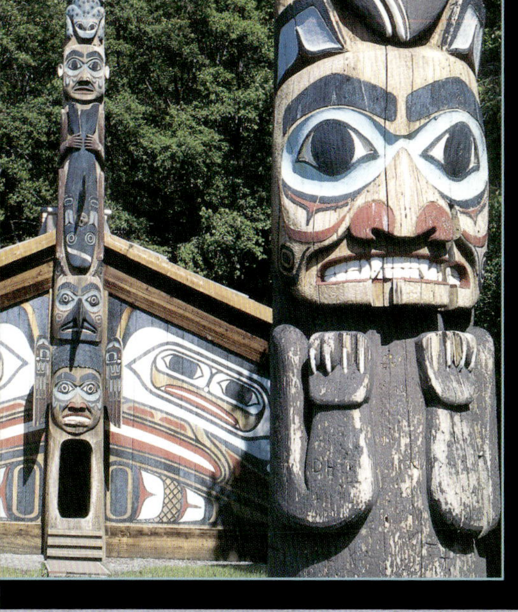

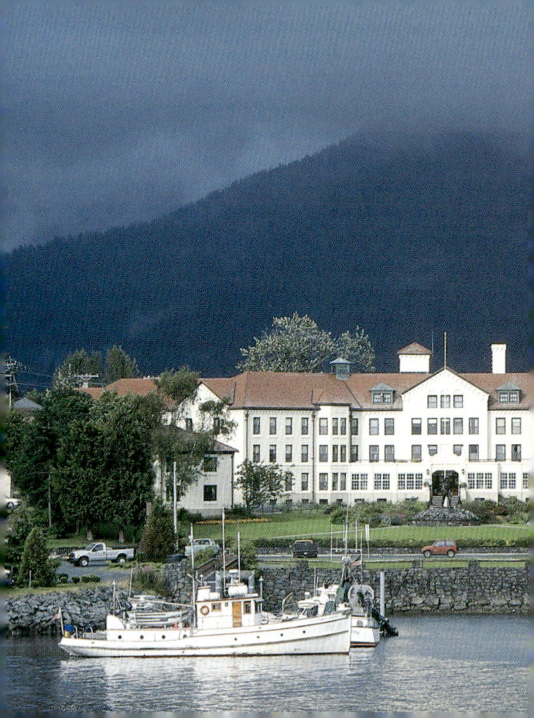

The Sitka Pioneer Home, near St Michael's Cathedral, was the first of six pioneer homes built in Alaska.

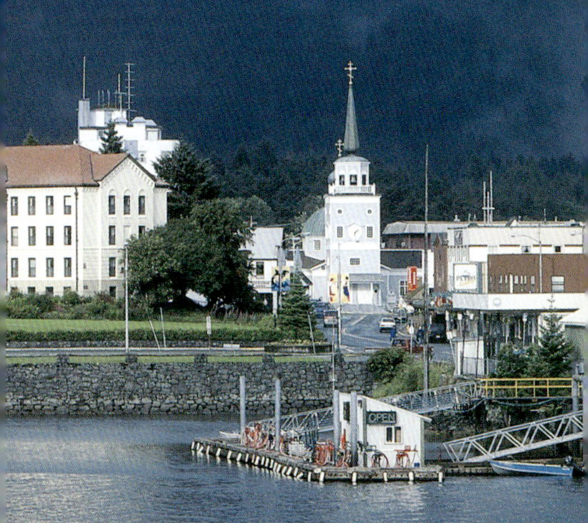

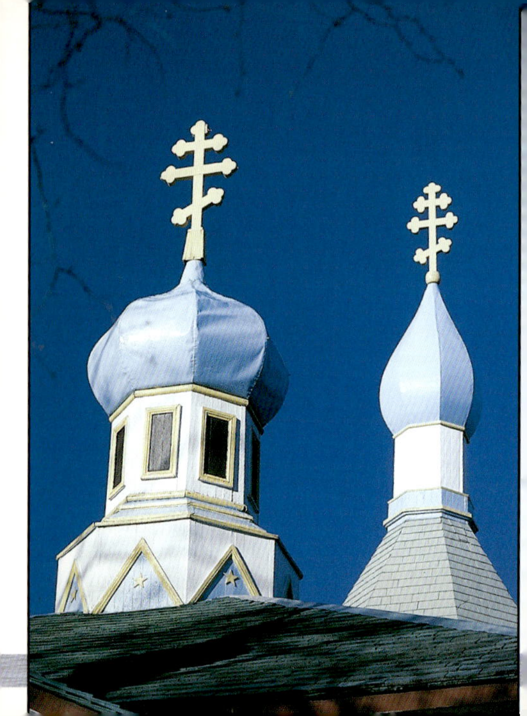

In 1799 Russia established an outpost in Sitka, which later became the Russian capital for Alaska. One result of these settlements can be seen today in the distinctive architecture of Russian Orthodox churches.

Holy Assumption Church.

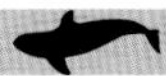

Replica of Sitka Russian blockhouse originally constructed in 1824.

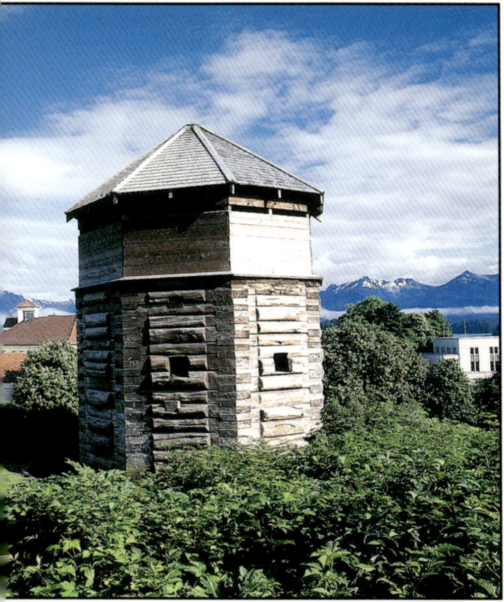

Silhouette of Russian Orthodox Church with Mount Redoubt in distance

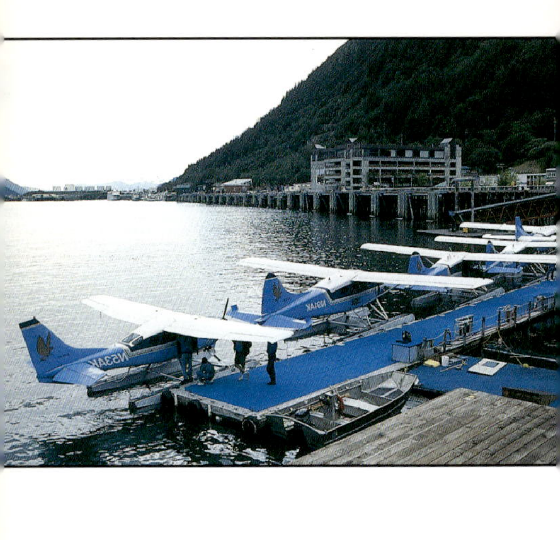

Juneau is the capital of Alaska. Arriving and leaving Juneau is by boat, plane, dog sled or snowmobile. There are no roads into and out of the city.

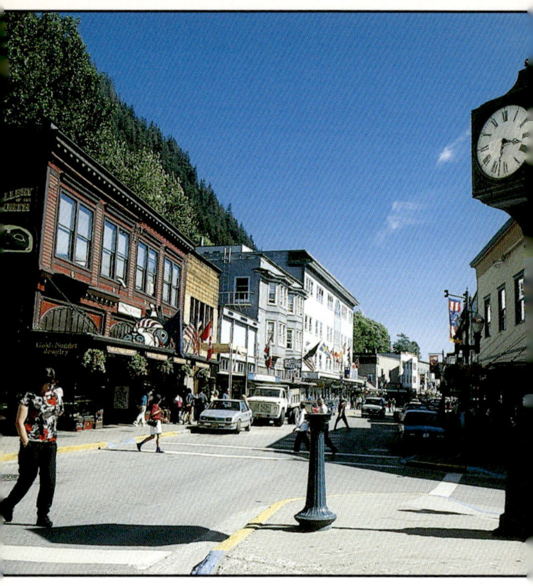

Front & Main Streets in Juneau. Robin Brandt

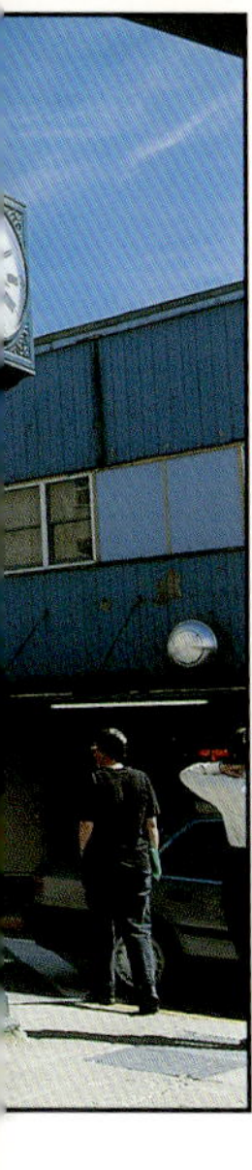

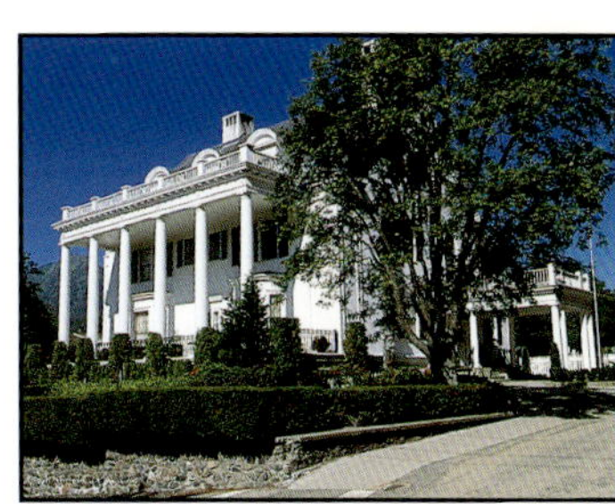

The Governor's Mansion in Juneau.
Robin Brandt

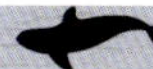

"I look forward to an America, which will not be afraid of grace and beauty, which will protect the beauty of our natural environment."

John F. Kennedy

Waterfall in Tracy Arm Fjord.

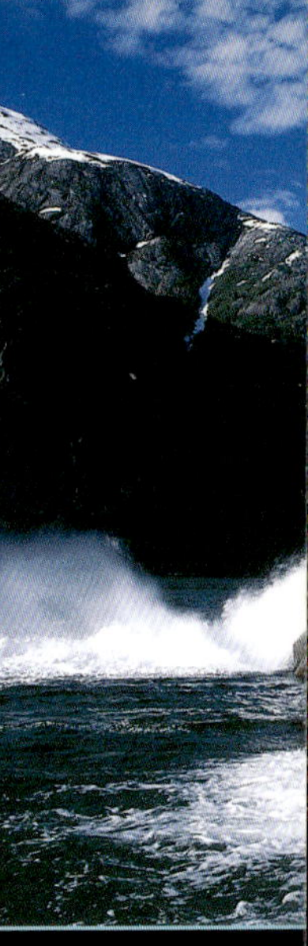

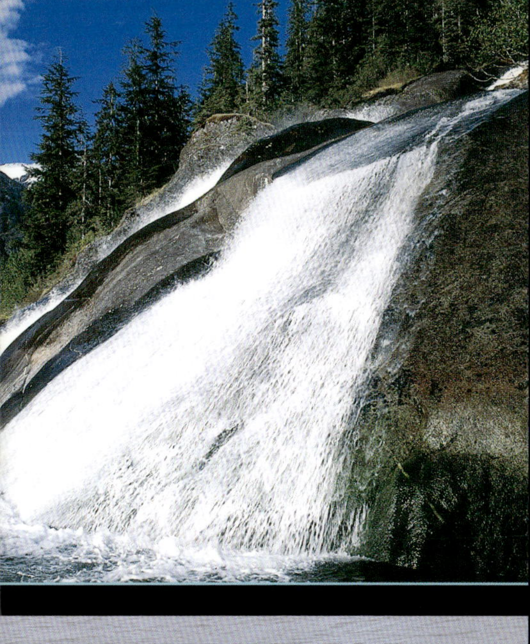

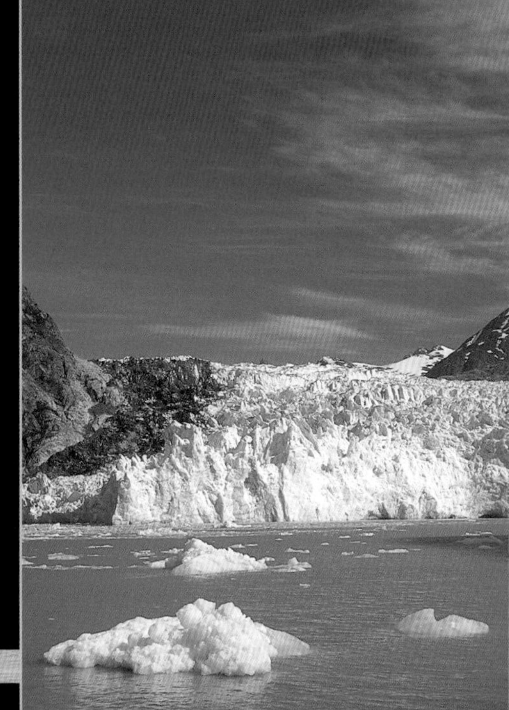

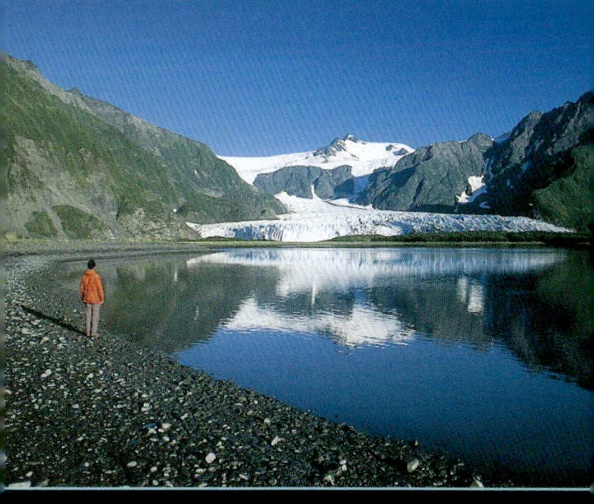

South Sawyer Glacier.
Penderson Glacier in Kenai Fjords National Park.

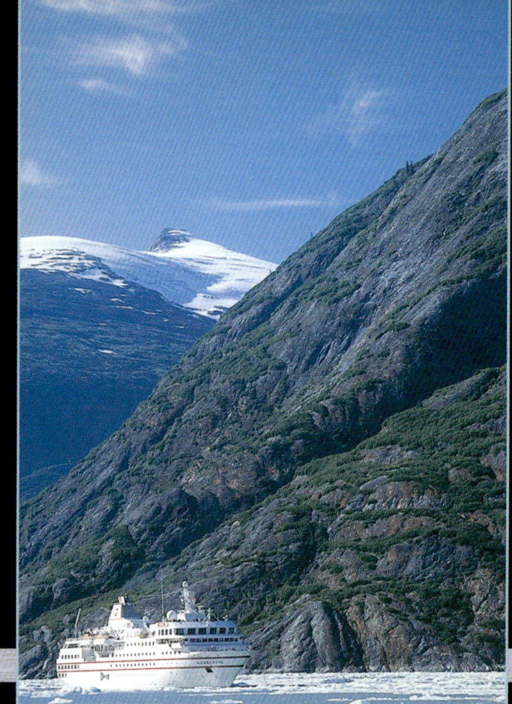

"Wilderness is an anchor to windward. Knowing it is there, we can also know that we are still a rich nation, tending our resources as we should."

Clinton P. Anderson

Cruise ship in Tracy Arm Fjord.

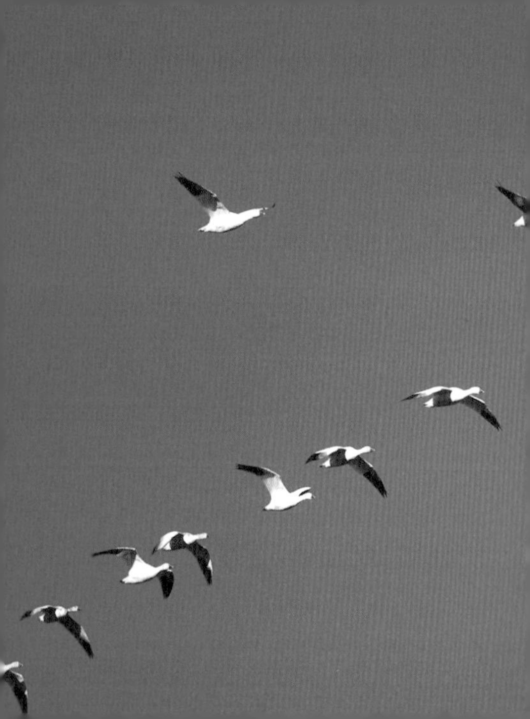

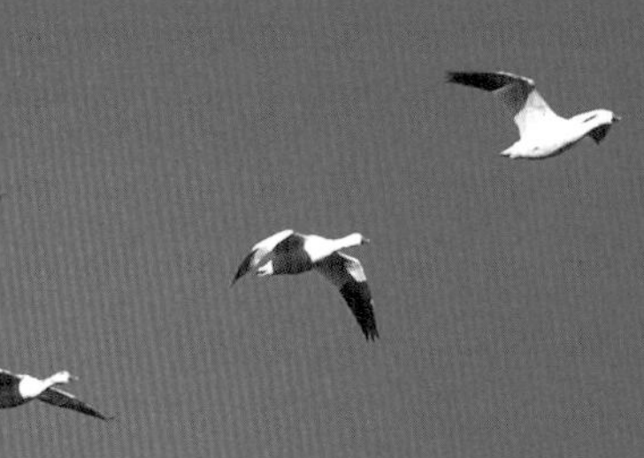

"If I were to name my three most precious resources of life, I should say books, friends and nature; and the greatest of these is nature."

John Burroughs

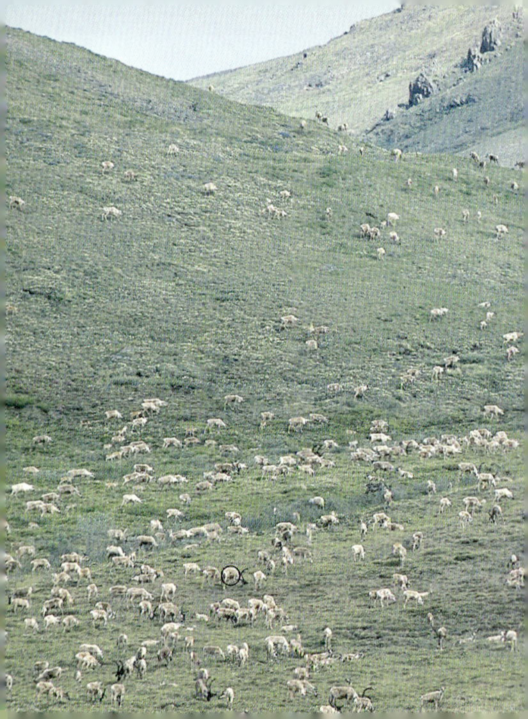

Sources

Clinton P. Anderson (1895-1975) U.S. Senator from New Mexico.

John Burroughs (1837-1921) U.S. author and naturalist. He traveled Alaska with the famous Harriman Expedition in 1899.

John F. Kennedy (1917-1963) 35th President of the United States.

John Muir (1939-1914) Conservationist, naturalist and explorer who wrote *Travels in Alaska* (1879) that prompted Americans to visit Alaska.

Adolph Murie (1889-1974) naturalist and author of several pioneering Alaska wildlife studies.

William Shakespeare (1564-1616) English poet and playwright. Quote is from *Troilus and Cressida*.

Henry David Thoreau (1817-1862) U.S. philosopher and author who lived his life respecting nature.

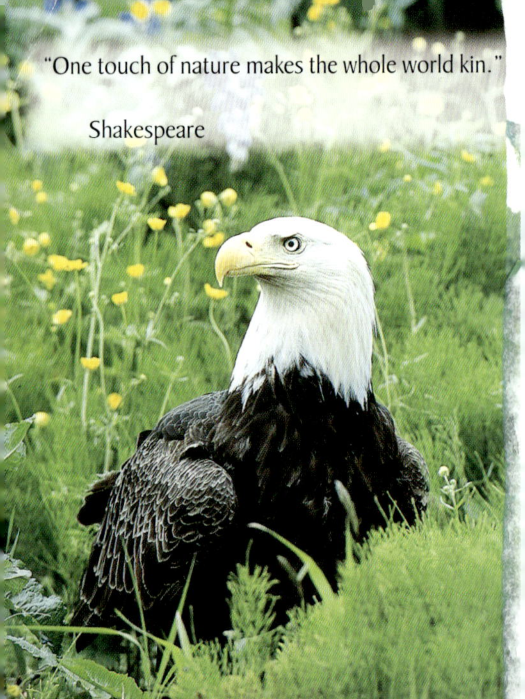
"One touch of nature makes the whole world kin."
Shakespeare